W9-AQI-462

2012

INFORMATION EXPLORER

SUPER SMART INFORMATION STRATEGIES

WONDERFUL WIKIS

by Ann Truesdell

MCL FOR NEPTUNE CITY PUBLIC LIBRARY

CHERRY LAKE PUBLISHING • ANN ARBOR, MICHIGAN

Published in the United States of America
by Cherry Lake Publishing
Ann Arbor, Michigan
www.cherrylakepublishing.com

Content Adviser: Gail Dickinson, PhD,
Associate Professor, Old Dominion University,
Norfolk, Virginia

Photo Credits: Cover, ©Media Bakery; page 4, ©Raywoo/Dreamstime.com; page 5, ©Ljupco Smokovski/Dreamstime.com; page 8, ©SergiyN/Shutterstock, Inc.; page 9, ©Monkey Business Images/Shutterstock, Inc.; page 10, ©Goodluz/Shutterstock, Inc.; page 11, ©wow/Shutterstock, Inc.; page 15, ©Monkey Business Images/Dreamstime.com; page 16, ©Ron Chapple/Dreamstime.com; page 17, ©Sergiy Nykonenko/Dreamstime.com; page 18, ©Malinhk/Dreamstime.com; page 22, ©Cuky/Dreamstime.com; page 23, ©Xalanx/Dreamstime.com; page 24, ©Dmitriy Shironosov/Shutterstock, Inc.; page 25, ©Pahham/Dreamstime.com; page 26, ©Lisa F. Young/Dreamstime.com; page 27, ©Jemiller/Dreamstime.com

Copyright ©2013 by Cherry Lake Publishing
All rights reserved. No part of this book may be reproduced or utilized in any form or by any means without written permission from the publisher.

Library of Congress Cataloging-in-Publication Data
Truesdell, Ann.
  Wonderful wikis / by Ann Truesdell.
      pages cm. — (Information explorer)
  Includes bibliographical references and index.
  ISBN 978-1-61080-480-6 (lib. bdg.) — ISBN 978-1-61080-654-1 (pbk.) — ISBN 978-1-61080-567-4 (e-book)
  1. Wikis (Computer science)—Juvenile literature. I. Title.
  TK5105.8882.T78 2013
  006.7'5—dc23   2012001758

Cherry Lake Publishing would like to acknowledge the work of The Partnership for 21st Century Skills. Please visit www.21stcenturyskills.org for more information.

Printed in the United States of America
Corporate Graphics Inc.
July 2012
CLFA11

A NOTE TO PARENTS AND TEACHERS: Please remind your children how to stay safe online before they do the activities in this book.

A NOTE TO KIDS: Always remember your safety comes first!

Table of Contents

CHAPTER ONE
What Is a Wiki?

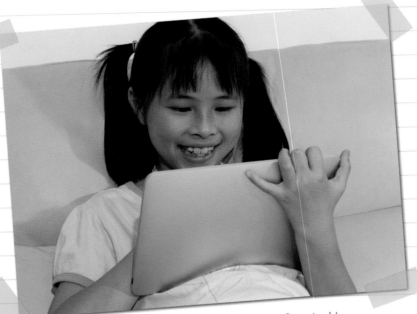

The Internet is a great source for both entertainment and useful information.

The Internet is an incredible way to learn new things. You have probably used it to research school projects. Maybe you have gone online to watch videos or read about sports, movies, or music. But the Internet is more than just a tool for looking up information. It also offers many ways to post information, or **content,** of your own for other people to see. Web sites called **wikis** are one of today's most popular ways to share content online. Millions of people around the world use these incredible Web sites to share information with one another.

A wiki is usually made up of many different pages. Each page contains information about a certain subject. Most Web sites only allow you to look at the content that has already been posted. You cannot make your own changes. But wikis are different. They allow you to add, delete, and edit content for other people to see. You might have extra information to add to what is already written on the wiki. Maybe you know of a great picture you could add to the page. These things can help make the page more useful for other people who look at it.

↑ Wikis let you share your thoughts with people all around the world.

TRY THIS!

Wikis are very popular on the Web. See if you can find a wiki that has been created by students your age. Type "class wiki" or "student-created wiki" into a search engine. Your search results should give you plenty of wikis to choose from.

Browse through three different wikis. Make some notes about the ways they are similar to and different from regular Web sites. Then answer some of the following questions:

- What subjects do the wikis cover?
- Do they offer pictures or videos?
- Are there links to other Web sites?
- Are there a lot of spelling mistakes on the wikis?
- Do they seem to provide useful information?
- Do you see Edit buttons anywhere on the wiki pages?
- What do these wikis have in common with other Web sites you have visited?
- How are these wikis different from other Web sites you have visited?

To get a copy of this activity, visit www.cherrylakepublishing.com/activities.

Wikis are a great tool for class projects.

Like other Web sites, wikis contain words, pictures, videos, and sound clips. Most also share links to other Web sites. The first difference you might notice between wikis and other Web sites is that wikis usually have an Edit button somewhere on each page. This makes it quick and easy for people to make changes to that page.

Did any of the wikis you visited during the activity look more like a rough draft than a final copy? Were there spelling mistakes or other errors? If so, this is because wikis are almost always changing. A wiki page is never really finished, because anyone can edit it at any time. This means that some wikis you visit might be more up-to-date than other Web sites. But not all wikis have the latest information. Always check to see when the wiki was last updated.

Many wikis are created for people to learn, both by posting what they know and having others add to what they posted. Sometimes teachers might offer lessons or responses to their students on a wiki. Sometimes students use wikis to combine their research for a group project. Read on to see how to make a wiki work for you.

The word wiki is a Hawaiian word meaning "fast" or "quick." It's a good name for this type of Web site because changing the content of a wiki is quick and easy. Most other kinds of Web sites take much more time to create or edit.

CHAPTER TWO
Why Use a Wiki?

↑ People of all ages use wikis to learn and share ideas.

A wiki can be a very powerful tool, especially for learning. It allows you to continue working whether you are at home or at school. It is good for working alone or in a group. Wikis are very popular among people of all ages, from kids to adults. Let's consider how you can use a wiki to make learning easier and more interesting.

All you need to create and edit a wiki page is a computer and a connection to the Internet. You do not need

You can work on a wiki anywhere that you have Internet access.

any special programs or equipment. This means that you can use a computer at school to start work on a wiki. Then you can finish up the work at home. You could work on your wiki at a library or even using a smartphone! This gives you almost endless options for working on a wiki. Some teachers even ask their students to turn in their homework by posting a file or editing a wiki page.

Wikis are easy to use from anywhere. Because of this, many students use them as a place to gather and store class notes, information for projects, videos, pictures, and more. A wiki can be used the way you might use a binder to organize your papers and projects. You might try taking notes or typing up essays on a wiki page. Imagine how interesting and complete your class notes could be with pictures and video! You can even use links to keep track of other Web sites with useful information.

Let's take it up a notch! A wiki becomes even more useful when many people are working on it. Your friends will love wikis for **collaboration**, or working together to create something. Many people can contribute to the same wiki page. Each person can add or change the information on the wiki. This allows you to learn from your friends while teaching them new things yourself.

People don't have to be in the same place to add to the wiki. They also don't have to make changes at

Wikis turn out better when more people work on them.

the same time. You will be able to see what your part-
ners have added, deleted, and changed as soon as they
do it. Because a wiki is never finished, you can keep
changing and adding to it whenever you need to. Many
wikis have a discussion board that lets you send mes-
sages back and forth to other people using the wiki.
You might use the discussion board to brainstorm ideas
together, ask each other questions, or make comments
on what others have posted. This means that you can
discuss things about the work on the page without actually changing anything on the page.

Students are not the only people who
use wikis. Many professionals use wikis
for the same reasons students do.
Even the Central Intelligence Agency
(CIA) has a wiki that its members use
to collect secret information. The CIA
wiki is called Intellipedia. It allows CIA
agents to share important discoveries
with each other. Because of the types
of information the agents share,
Intellipedia is password protected!

TRY THIS!

As you now know, a wiki is a great tool for collaboration. One person can begin a page, and other people can edit it and add to it.

Before you create a wiki online, get some friends together and practice by using a sheet of paper.

Practice Wiki

Practice Wiki! Soccer

1. Decide on a topic that everyone in the group knows about. You might choose a sport, television show, or type of music.
2. Ask each member to think of some facts they know about the topic.
3. Have one group member write down a couple of facts about the topic.

Practice Wiki Soccer

continue on the next page

CONTINUED

4. Pass the paper to the next group member. This person can add new facts about the topic. He or she might also change things that the first group member wrote, in order to make the wiki better.

5. Continue passing the paper around until everyone has added information.

What did you like about collaborating? Did your group members teach you anything new? How would the project be different if you could add pictures, video, audio, and links? Was there anything you didn't like about collaborating? Did any group members disagree with the changes? Collaboration is not always easy, but we often know more as a group than we do alone.

To get a copy of this activity, visit www.cherrylakepublishing.com/activities.

CHAPTER THREE

Working on Wikis

Many teachers set up wikis for their students to use.

Are you interested in working on a wiki? If you are under 13 years old, you will probably need permission from a parent or teacher to create your own at sites such as www.wikispaces.com. You might be lucky enough to have a class wiki that you can use. You can also work on other wikis that you find online.

Each wiki has its own set of **permissions**. Permissions are the different ways that people are

Ask a parent if you need help setting up a new wiki.

able to access a wiki. A private wiki means that only certain people can view and edit it. Protected wikis often let anyone view the wiki, but only people with a password can edit it.

A public wiki is the most open type of wiki. It allows anyone to view and edit all pages. Some wikis are made up of a mix of private, protected, and public pages. To get started on a private or protected wiki, you might have to sign up to become a member. Each member receives a username and password so he or she can log in and edit the wiki.

Once you are on a wiki, you can edit an existing page or create a new page. Most wikis have a

navigation section with links to many of the major pages. Plus, there is usually a Search box that lets you search the site using keywords. Some wiki pages may even have a table of contents to help you find your way through a long page.

The best part about a wiki is that adding content is so easy. Once you have the right page on your screen, editing is often as simple as clicking a button. Each wiki page should have its own Edit button. Click this button to edit the page.

Changing or adding additional content to a wiki page is a simple, easy process.

You can take your
own digital videos
and add them to
wiki pages.

You can add to the content, delete parts of it, or change things already on it. A **toolbar** might show up after you click the Edit button. The toolbar has many buttons that help you to change other things on the page. For example, some buttons might let you change the style, size, or color of the text on the page.

The toolbar also gives you the option of adding links, pictures, videos, or files to the page. You can upload files to the wiki from your computer. You can also **embed** files from other sites. Embedding lets you add videos, images, or other files you find online without saving them to your computer first. Your wiki toolbar should also have the important Save button. Be sure to click it when you are done editing so that your work will be posted online.

Another important wiki feature is the **history**. The history allows you to view older versions of each page on the wiki. You can see how and when other users changed the wiki. The history may also let you **revert**, or go back, to an older version of the page. This can be very useful if you or another user make a mistake while editing the wiki.

One feature that many wikis do not yet have is a spell-checker. Are you concerned about spelling on your wiki? If so, you may want to type your words into a program that does have a spell-checker, such as a word processor. After you have checked your spelling, copy and paste your words into your wiki.

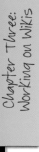

TRY THIS!

The most famous wiki on the Internet is Wikipedia. Wikipedia is an online encyclopedia that anyone can edit. Tens of thousands of people regularly contribute to this wiki. They add information and keep an eye on topics that they are experts in, to make sure everything is correct. Millions of visitors read articles on the site every day. It is a wonderful example of collective knowledge. There is more information on Wikipedia than could ever fit into a printed encyclopedia. Best of all, it is free to use!

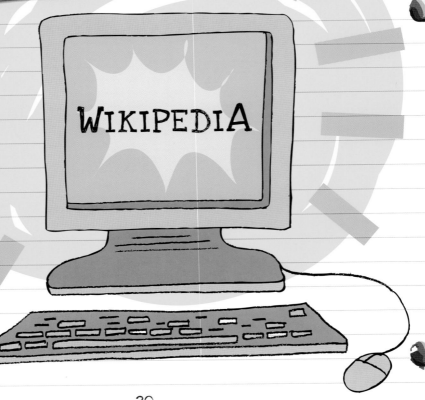

WIKIPEDIA

Let's take a look at Wikipedia and see what features it has to offer. Go to www.wikipedia.org. Search for an article about your hometown. Then take a look at the following features:

- Edit button
- Toolbar (when in Edit mode)
- Save button (when in Edit mode)
- History of page changes
- Table of contents for the page
- Links to other Web sites
- References and citations to show where the information was originally found
- Discussion boards
- Pictures
- Search bar

Chicago 🔍

READ | EDIT | VIEW HISTORY

What did you find? How does it compare to other wikis you have visited? Find a Wikipedia article about your state or province. How does it compare to the article about your hometown?

To get a copy of this activity, visit www.cherrylakepublishing.com/activities.

CHAPTER FOUR
Following the Rules

Following the rules will help keep you safe and improve the quality of your wiki.

Working on a wiki often means working with other people. This means that you have to keep in mind many of the same rules you follow when working with people face-to-face.

The content you post on a wiki might be information that you found using another source. You probably already know that it is important to **cite** your sources when you write a paper for school. It is just as important to cite your sources when you post information online. When you tell where you got your content, you are giving credit to the original authors or owners of that work. Luckily, this can be done quite easily on a wiki. It is as simple as copying and pasting a link to the Web site where you found the information.

You also have to be responsible about posting personal information on a wiki. There are many ways to stay safe on the Web. The best way is to keep specific information about yourself private.

Be sure to cite your sources. It is against the law to use other people's work without giving them credit.

Never post your full name or address. Many people even avoid giving their first name or any location besides their country. You might come up with a **screen name** instead of using your real name.

You are sure to receive feedback when you post on a wiki. Do you allow anyone to see and edit your page? If so, people might talk about your content on the wiki discussion board or even right on the wiki

Ask an adult for help if you aren't sure which kinds of information you should share online.

Use feedback to figure out your wiki's weaknesses and make them better.

page. Feedback comes in many different forms. Some people might mention the things they liked about your page. Others might write about mistakes you made. This does not mean that you've done a bad job with your wiki. These people are simply pointing out places where you can improve. These comments can actually be very helpful. No matter how good your wiki is, there is always something you can do to improve it. This is perhaps the greatest power of your wiki!

Don't be surprised if someone else edits your wiki page. That is what wikis are all about!

You should also remember that unless your page is private or protected, anyone can edit your page! Some people might add content to your page to expand on what is already there. They might also delete or change some of your work. Most people who edit your wiki page are only trying to make it better. If someone does ruin your page, the history can bring back your older work. Do you disagree with something that another person has done to your page? Start a discussion with that person to figure out what is best for the wiki.

Whenever you edit a wiki, make sure that you are doing something to improve the page. If you make a big change, it is polite to post a comment to the discussion board that explains why you changed what you did. Make sure that the comments or questions you post on the discussion board are helpful and polite. Be careful not to hurt anyone's feelings when you edit wiki pages that others have created. When you make changes or post comments, be aware that real people will read your words. Think about how they will feel when they see the page.

Be sure to treat people online with the same courtesy you do face-to-face. ↳

TRY THIS!

When you visit a wiki, think about how you might improve it. You may know some facts that could be added to the information already there. You may find information that is incorrect or worded in a way that doesn't make sense.

Let's practice making changes to a document. Read the paragraph below. What information could you add? What information is confusing? How can you change the confusing parts to make it better? Is there something that you would delete? If you change something, consider how you would explain your changes on a discussion board.

To get a copy of this activity, visit www.cherrylakepublishing.com/activities.

Cats are interesting creatures. They have four legs, plus a tail. Some people keep them as pets. However, they cannot be kept as a pet if they are too big. Cats have nine lives.

You might make the following additions and changes to the paragraph:

Cats are interesting creatures. They are mammals, and they have four legs, plus a tail. Some people keep domesticated cats as pets. However, large cats like lions, tigers, and jaguars are wild animals and cannot be kept as pets. ~~Cats have nine lives.~~

You might then leave the following note on the wiki page's discussion board to explain your changes:

- The part about cats being kept as pets was a little confusing, so I tried to make it more clear.
- I deleted the sentence "Cats have nine lives" because it is not a fact. It is just a thing that people say. It means that cats can fall or jump from high places and often land without hurting themselves. But that makes me wonder...how long do cats usually live?

Is there a topic that you would like to learn more about? Or maybe you already consider yourself an expert on a topic. It's time for you to visit a wiki. Maybe you will even create one of your own! Combine learning and sharing, and you will learn even more.

Glossary

cite **(SITE)** give credit to a source

collaboration **(kuh-lab-uh-RAY-shun)** working together to create something

content **(KON-tent)** the information included on Web sites, such as words, pictures, videos, and audio files

embed **(im-BED)** to place outside content into a Web site

history **(HISS-tur-ee)** a feature on many wikis that lets users view a record of the changes made to each page

navigation **(nav-uh-GAY-shun)** the act of finding your way around

permissions **(pur-MIH-shunz)** restrictions on who can edit or view certain wiki pages

revert **(rih-VURT)** to return something to the way it was in the past

screen name **(SKREEN NAYM)** a name that someone uses on the Internet, often instead of using his or her real name

toolbar **(TOOL-bar)** a menu bar that appears when editing a wiki page

wikis **(WIH-keez)** Web sites that allow multiple users to edit their pages

Find Out More

BOOKS

Anderson, Jennifer Joline. *Wikipedia: The Company and Its Founders*. Edina, MN: ABDO, 2011.

Cornwall, Phyllis. *Online Etiquette and Safety*. Ann Arbor, MI: Cherry Lake Publishing, 2010.

Pascaretti, Vicki, and Sara Wilkie. *Team Up Online*. Ann Arbor, MI: Cherry Lake Publishing, 2010.

WEB SITES

Wikipedia

http://en.wikipedia.org/wiki/Main_Page

Visit the most famous wiki on the Internet.

Wikispaces

www.wikispaces.com

Create a free wiki of your own.

Index

About the Author

Ann Truesdell is a school library media specialist and teacher in Michigan. She and her husband, Mike, love traveling and spending time with their children, James and Charlotte.